To the "greig girls"
with ♡
Shari +
12/1/98

Benjy

Benjamin's World

Author ~ Shari Nocks Gladstone
Illustrator ~ Candace Staulcup

Revised Edition

Biographical Publishing Company
Prospect, Connecticut

Benjamin's World

Revised Edition

Published by:

Biographical Publishing Company
35 Clark Hill Road
Prospect, CT 06712-1011
Phone: 203-758-3661   e-mail: biopub@aol.com

Library of Congress Cataloging-in-Publication Data
Gladstone, Shari Nocks, 1930-
Benjamin's World / Shari Nocks Gladstone :
    illustrated by Candace Staulcup. — Rev. ed.
    p. cm.
ISBN 0-9637240-1-0 (alk. paper)
    1. Cats — Literary collections.   I. Title.
PS3557.L2918B46 1998
    813'.54 — dc21   98-8429
                                                              CIP

Contents

FOREWORD 5

THE KITTEN 10

GIMME A BREAK! 16

MAGNOLIA 26

THE FENCE 30

I'M A BIG BOY NOW — 42

LONELINESS 50

A WINTER DAY 56

WHEN LILI CAME 65

LILI'S STORY 74

AFTERWORD 84

PUSSY CAT HEAVEN - - - an addendum 91

Foreword

I guess every story has a beginning: some special thought, idea or happenstance that starts plot and characters coming to life in the author's mind. Perhaps, for me, it began when Jim brought a little kitten into our house to alleviate my grief over a loved but ailing animal. But it really all came together some time later.

As you probably know, a wise pet owner does not allow a new kitten out of the house until a suitable period of "bonding" has taken place. This generally coincides with the completion of a series of immunization shots recommended by any responsible veterinarian and about the time the little furry thing has been in residence for at least a month or six

weeks. Going Out For The First Time becomes, then, a big deal.

On Benjamin's First Day Out he was soon drunk with fresh air, bird and squirrel watching, butterfly chasing, and the investigation of bugs, ants and all other things that crawl. I was watching the little bit of fluff like a hawk, knowing he was too ignorant of the ways of the world to get out of trouble, should trouble come his way. A household task took me indoors for no longer than two minutes, but in that small amount of time, I lost track of the little guy. I was frantic and called, whistled, hissed and visually searched, to no avail. He was, to all appearances, gone.

Suddenly, a movement in the bushes caught my eye. There was Benjamin, His Royal Tininess, seemingly The Kitten In Charge at his first formal meeting with the Three Big Tomcats Who Live Next Door. Only a fraction of their size, he sat bolt upright facing the others. He stared at them and they stared at him. It looked to me as if messages were passing between them. Important messages. Without a doubt they were communicating, though what was being said was not in a language that I am privileged to understand.

That's when my mind really went to work, and the "Benjamin" stories began to take shape. My head filled with anecdotes, based on what I could see of his daily life, but narrated from the kitten's point of view. As I watched him grow and develop, have a variety of experiences and make all kinds of discoveries, I imagined the chronicling of his thoughts, as I believed they might have evolved. And, though I do not know the arcane Feline language he thinks in, I translated it to what I know — and to the few "people" words that Benjamin and I have agreed to share.

A year has passed. Benjamin has experienced trauma and death and finally maturity. He is an almost-adult cat. To tell the truth, he is indulged and pampered. He appears to be daring, but is a wimp at heart. Most of the time, his curiosity gets him into trouble. He swaggers forth bravely, but quickly runs for cover and relies on his People to save him when he is frightened or in trouble.

He is currently waging a war of persistence with Jim over who has first-and-only rights to the bed, the sunny part of the kitchen table and a few mutually favored chairs. (So far, Jim appears to be losing.)

The stories that follow are in sequence. Benjamin gets older, and wiser, as they progress. His knowledge and vocabulary increase. (Actually, much of his story is told in Kitten Thought — but I'm sure you'll understand every word of it.) At the end of his saga, he has figured out a lot of things. He finally knows the boundaries of his life and of his world. He is devoted to his People and is, in both fact and fiction, the most loving of creatures.

Shari Nocks Gladstone
Dix Hills, N. Y.
1991

The Kitten

There they were — two old folks, an old dog and an old cat. Just the four of them in the big yellow house. They had been together for a long time. Neat. Quiet. Sedentary. Set in their ways.

The skinny old man had difficulty breathing, complained a lot and rarely laughed. The chubby old lady read continuously and did as little physical activity as was possible. The old dog was stiff and arthritic, and rarely romped as he once used to do. The old cat was truly neurotic. She choked up hairballs all over the place, and, if the truth be known, on occasion she had begun to ignore the litter box. She was so ritualistic that her needs and moods controlled the other three.

Breakfast at 6 AM. Snacks at 4 PM. Milk at 9 PM. In her own dish. In her special place. On her own terms.

But, that was the way of it. The four old beings — two with skin and two with fur — respected each others' space, followed their rigid routines and accommodated each others' whims. That was their life.

Then there came a day when it was time for the cat to go to the vet. In fact the scheduled visit was long overdue. This seemed to be such a difficult task that the old woman was inclined to delay as long as possible. But, there had to be shots. And the cat's toenails were so long they were growing into her footpads. Furthermore, she had a terrible odor. It couldn't be put off another day.

What bad news! The vet found an enormous tumor in the cat's ear. It was the source of the noxious odor. The old woman demurred when the vet suggested surgery.

"I always promised her that there would never be any pain."

"But," said the vet, "I think I can get it

out. Maybe we can buy her some time. She deserves the chance — if only she can survive the anesthesia."

The next few days were long and gray. The old woman was morose. In her heart she believed her companion of 15 years would be gone. "At her age" she thought, "she'll never survive." Even when the vet said, after the surgery, that it looked as if she might make it, the old lady's inner voice said, "She'll never be the same again. Maybe I should have put her to sleep. Maybe I should have spared her the pain. She's never been away from me before. She must feel so alone."

She was as sad as she had ever been.

The old man had, for years, said that he hated cats and was allergic to them. He had said, many more times than once, "When this one goes, there'll never be another cat in this house."

The old lady, remembering, said "How will I live the rest of my life without a kitty?"

But, some weeks ago, at his daughter's house in another town, the old man had seen a litter of kittens being born out in the woods.

When he visited, from time to time, he saw how they were growing. He admired how they managed to survive, even though they had no real home and were living outdoors in the dank, rainy weather of early Spring. Somehow one of those half-wild things (the little striped male with the white face and the white tip on his tail) came home in his raincoat pocket. When the world seemed darkest for the old woman, a tiny pink nose touched her hand. A sandpaper tongue licked her fingers. Soft paws touched her face. Needle sharp teeth nibbled at her ear lobe.

Well, what happened after that?

The old cat didn't die. She came home from the vet on the same day the kitten had his first shots. There was feline mayhem in the car as they all drove home together. Weighing less than two pounds, the kitten entered the household and became part of the family — and nothing was ever the same again.

The old man still dozes in his chair — but with the kitten in his lap. His allergies seem to have disappeared. He is rarely without a smile as he makes ingenious kitten toys out of balls of twine and bits of paper. And he says to the old lady, "Well, did he get his vitamins today?"

The old lady dashes here and there. To the pet store for special food. To the library for a book on cat care. To the vet for his latest advice. To a friend's house to show off new photos. She is simply everywhere.

The old dog doesn't stop wagging his long black tail — and yelps with pleasure when the kitten chases it. And catches it. And swings on it.

The old cat never looked better. She spends her time watching the little bit of striped gray fluff as he plays his kitten games. She folds her paws under her chest and purrs as the kitten chases her. Jumps on her. Eats out of her dish. Drinks her milk. Messes up her litter box. Takes over her favorite chair. Once in a while she swats at him with a forepaw, probably just for his own good.

The floor is strewn with the contents of overturned wastepaper baskets. The couch pillows are disarranged. Pilfered yarn decorates the staircase. Kitty toys — the good kind with catnip and bells inside — are all over the place. There are new rules. Neatness no longer seems as important as it used to be.

Quiet reading is a thing of the past. Doors that used to be closed are open. Visitors stop by daily to see the new member of the family.

And four old beings — two with skin and two with fur — exchange side-long glances. The humans say, "Where's the kitten?" and ask each other "He's not getting into trouble, is he?" They nudge each other, making a point of sharing each new antic. Each new trick.

It looks as if one little kitten has given them all a new lease on life.

Gimme A Break!

Hey, you big guys, gimme a break! I'm only three months old. Actually, today's my birthday and, to tell the truth, I still don't even know how to meow exactly right. (Sometimes, especially when I'm tryin' real hard, it just comes out like a squeak!) When you get right down to it, there's so much I don't know how to do yet, and so much I've still got to check out and investigate, I'm simply overwhelmed. I've got so much I need to learn about life. I think I need some help!

My name is Benjy and I'm a Tom Cat. Well, maybe I'm still just a kitten, but I'll be a Tom someday. I only weigh four and a half pounds — at least that's what I heard my People say. That sounds OK to me, even though I'm not sure what "pounds" are or what "four and a half" means, either. But, if it's OK with them, it's OK with me.

I've got some important stuff to deal with. I've got waste baskets to climb into and dump over. I've got big paper bags from the supermarket to get inside of and hide. I've got crumpled balls of shiny foil to chase. I've got balls and balls of yarn to unravel. (Right now I'm workin' on a big basketful over there by the fireplace!) I've got electric cords to gnaw on and lots of fancy stuff on the table to sniff at and push around.

And I've got a Feline Senior Citizen and a Canine Senior Citizen that need looking after. If I don't get them up 'n' doing a few times a day, they'll just be lazin' around, sleepin' all the time and doin' nothin' while I've got so much to keep me busy.

Doesn't seem fair, does it?

I've got places under tables and chairs that nobody's been into in ages. (Some real good dust bunnies there. Interestin' the way they stick to my whiskers!) I've got curtains to climb on, cushions to scratch, mouse holes to check out and Humans to cuddle. What responsibilities! Where is a kitten like me supposed to find the time to handle all this

stuff?

Gimme a break!

And when I go outside, there are birds and bugs and moths and fireflies. When I see them my teeth fairly chatter! I know I'm supposed to try to act cool and aloof, like one of you big guys, but I get so excited, sometimes I try to chase them all at the same time. Jumpin' here and jumpin' there. Fallin' all over myself. Wow!

(Ya know, once in a while when I'm Attackin' the Enemy, and when I'm playin' my Tiger-in-the-Jungle game, I think my People are laughin' at me. Could that be?)

But, if the truth be known, it's not the wastebaskets and the mouse holes and the fireflies that keep me runnin'. It's my Humans. As much as I love them, I really don't understand them too good yet. Let me tell you what happened yesterday. You'll never believe it!

My Mother Person is soft and cuddly and likes to cook. She was doing something fancy with a chicken at the kitchen counter. Of course, I felt it was my job to help her — so up

I jumped, checked it out (and, if the truth be known) snitched a yummy piece of chicken. It was kinda fun.

Well, she's usually pretty gentle, but this time she put me down on the floor with a thump. I didn't like that too much so I jumped up again. And she plopped me down again. It went on like that for awhile 'til she got very angry at me. (I'm not really sure why she got so mad, but she sure did!)

Then she yelled at me:

"Benjy is a bad, bad kitty!"

And she shook her finger in my face. Now, even tho' I'm still kinda little, I know that's something we macho Cats just don't tolerate. Well, I showed her. I put my tail up as high up as I could, turned my back to her and walked away. I'd show her what's what! (Besides, she'd already put the chicken away in the 'figerator!) So I ran up and down the stairs a few times, makin' my feet thump real loud like I was some kinda monster. But, nobody paid any attention to me.

Then I ran up and down the hall and did some of my best jumps. Ya know — the kind only kittens can do — goin' about a foot straight up in the air with all four paws off the ground at the same time. Then I did a series of Buckin' Bronco Loop-The-Loops and two complete Tumble-Overs. (That takes a lot of effort, ya know!)

Nobody paid any attention to me 'cept for the Senior Canine. He watched me and sorta whimpered, the way they do. So I arched my back into my best Halloween Kitty Trick, and I hissed, and I spit, and I even tried to make Big Tail. (Well, it actually doesn't get too big yet, but I thought it was kind of impressive, considerin'!) The old dog just went back to sleep. Was I being ignored, or what? I used up all my energy, doin' all my best stuff, and nobody seemed to care. What a bummer!

Well, when all is said and done, it just seemed to be the right time for a nap. I found a spot on a shelf in the sun and curled up in a round wooden thing that smelled garlicky good. In minutes, I was off in dreamland.

I guess a few hours went by. Suddenly there was a lot of excitement. I heard doors slammin', drawers openin' and closin', stuff thumpin' around, and voices callin' me:

"Benjy. Where are you?" and "Pssst! Pssst!" (Ya know, that funny noise Humans make, hissin' through their teeth when they want you to come to them in a big hurry.) Well, after the way she treated me, I wasn't goin' anywhere in a hurry! I just stayed real quiet and invisible, the way we do — ya know?

My Mother Person kept callin' and callin'. She sounded a little upset, but I remembered the way she plopped me down, and hurt my feelin's — so I didn't move a whisker or stir a paw.

Then, the Father Person got into the act. I heard him ask, "Do you think he's stuck somewhere? Or hurt? Or lost?"

I began to think it over. Hmmm. Maybe he really cares about me.

"Should I look outside," he asked. "Maybe he's up a tree and can't get down."

"Omigod!" said the Mother Person. "I'm so upset I could cry! I don't know what I'd do if we ever lost him."

Well, that's more like it. That's what I like to hear. Maybe they really do love me, even if I am naughty from time to time. Sometimes I just can't help it. Sometimes there's so much I don't understand about what's good and what's bad that it all gets pretty confusin'. I guess I'll just have to keep on tryin' 'til I get it all straight. Well, for now, I think I'll just wiggle a little, and make some kinda noises. Then see what happens.

"Did you hear that?" she said. (She has sharper ears than he does — almost as good as mine!)

"No" he said. "I didn't hear anything. Let me look down in the basement." I wiggled a little bit more.

"What's that?"

Now they both heard me. The poked into everythin' — pullin' out pots, pans, dishes and what all and puttin' them on the floor. I stuck my head up, high as I could. The sunlight was shinin' on my whiskers.

"Look, look!! There on the shelf. He's in the old salad bowl! Omigod! We've found him."

She held me and cuddled me and

scratched my tummy. He rubbed my ears the way I like it 'til — I just couldn't help it — I gave in and purred and purred and purred.

"Who'd a thought," he said.

"In the salad bowl." she wondered, shaking her head.

"Isn't he just the little dickens!" he answered.

Well, I guess you guys think I'm a real push-over — givin' in and lettin' myself get found so quick. And purrin' so loud. And gettin' all kinda babyish and cuddley — ya know. All that gooey stuff.

But I did it 'cause my Father Person is sort of special and I couldn't let him get all fussed. Since I know him, and it's not been all that long, he's saved my life more than once. There was the first time that I went up the tree and couldn't get down. He just reached up and got me. Then, the next time, I went up so high that I couldn't come down for nothin'. I was really stuck. I stayed out almost all night and got so scared and cried and cried, 'til he got a ladder and came up and got me, and carried me down inside his shirt.

And, just the other day when the big dog from down the street, with the long drooly pink tongue and those enormous teeth — well I don't even want to think about that right now! But, anyway, he just scooped me up right in the nick of time. It's because of him — my very own Human Father Person — that my nine lives are still intact.

So, gimme a break! Sometimes a little guy's just gotta do what he's gotta do.

Magnolia

If I may say so, a lady of advanced years deserves a little respect! And that's the way things used to be around here. Now that that little upstart, Benjamin, is here — things are all turned around. Everything is topsy turvy. Why, I hardly know how to conduct my life properly.

In the old days — before Benjamin — we had a dignified catly routine. We had a time for everything, and a place for everything. A Lady Cat knew the rules and what was expected of her. And what she could expect of her People. Now, if I may say so, it's just mass confusion. It's hard to believe that one Minimal Feline could cause so much trouble.

For starters, I used to be able to get my breakfast at the correct hour — 6 AM — in peace and quiet. I would wait outside Mother

Person's bedroom door, doing some soft-morning-howling now and then to insure she would be awake exactly on time. It wasn't too difficult. She's usually pretty prompt. She would get out the can of food (Only the best brand, if you please!) and my bowl, and within seconds it was all set out for me on a special little table where The Dog couldn't reach it. I would eat — or sometimes pretend to be finicky and picky — to get some cuddling and petting, use the Sanitary Box, wash my face and my paws, and then go off to a sunny corner for a nap. And that was all there was to it.

Now, that little interloper, Benjy, wakes me up at the crack of dawn, jumping all over me, pouncing on me while I wait for Mother Person and just generally upsetting the whole process. He causes me to lose my temper. By the time 6 o'clock comes, I am virtually exhausted. Then, when we get in the kitchen, he is so excited by the idea of breakfast that he bites my tail, jumps on my head, goes up on my special table and eats out of the wrong bowl. Indeed, I have known him to take what is rightfully mine! He even — I am positively humiliated to admit — tries to eat the Dog Food! Since all actions have a reaction, that causes the Dog to gobble up whatever Feline

food he can get. What an ungodly mess! I have to eat so fast, and so much, to be sure that I get my share — I'm getting positively stout.

And, if you think that's bad, you better hear about what happens in the Sanitary Box. Mother Person was very considerate when Benjy arrived. He was really very little then, and hardly knew how to do these things correctly, so she got him a small, separate Box of his own. Well, the first thing the little upstart did was mess up MY BOX. Why couldn't he just use his own, and have done with it? But no — he messed up his box and my box and did everything the wrong way, leaving me to clean up after him, lest I have to Step In It. Yuch!

Some of this is simply too crude to discuss. I find I can't go on, without becoming actually bilious!

The Fence

Well, it looks as if I've gotten into awful trouble again. I just don't know why these things keep happenin' to me. It's a genuine wonderment!

Right now I'm sitting in the dark place under the sofa where nobody can find me, trying to get my thoughts together. Actually, I've had a simply turrible day. Just a few minutes ago my heart was beatin' faster than fast. I needed to calm my nerves, so I did an all-over bath. Then I extra washed my paws and the pretty white places on my ears and my face and my tummy and the tip of my tail. Then I did it all over again — but I'm still not calmed down. So I'll just sit here for awhile

all by myself and let the day turn into night.
And I'll keep thinkin' and thinkin'. Maybe I'll
come up with some answers.

Ya know, sometimes you start out doing somethin' that's really good fun — an adventure, like — and in the end it turns out to be somethin' that almost gets you killed. Quick as a flash, you can lose one of your nine lives without even realizin' it. Just like what happened to me earlier today.

Ya see, the Senior Canine in this house is very set in his ways. Every day, at the same time, he goes across the street and down the block to a little patch of trees where he takes care of his Personal Sanitary Business. (Now, frankly, I don't understand this at all. Why doesn't the poor old fella have a box at the bottom of the bathroom closet the way we self-respectin' Felines do? I know I would just hate it if I had to walk all the way down the block to take care of my Sanitary Business — not to mention, doin' it outside where anybody could see me. Wow!) But anyway, I really didn't know what he was up to, so I just followed along after him — and that's when all the trouble started.

It was a hot and sunny day, and we were out in the backyard. It's really sensational out there. It's my favorite place in the whole wide world. There's bushes and tall grass to play in, and lots of trees to climb. And there's bugs and moths to chase. And squirrels and mice and birds and all other kinds of stuff to keep you busy. And I was chasin' and runnin' and jumpin' like I'm s'posed to. Every so often, I make sure to run over and pounce on the Senior Canine and chase his tail, or somethin'. Just to keep him in the game, ya know. (Even tho' he growls at me once in a while, I know he loves it!)

So this one time, after climbin' four BIG trees in a row and comin' down backwards AND frontwards — which, I have to point out, most kittens my age can't nearly do — I hopped over to the Senior Canine just to check in. I pounced on him, jumpin' right outta the biggest bush, ya know, and trying my best to look real scary. That woke him up all right. He shook himself off and started to walk away, very slow like.

I just followed him, havin' nothin' better to do at the moment, until suddenly we weren't in the backyard anymore. We were someplace hot and hard that hurt my feet and where there wasn't any grass or trees. It's called The Street. (I know that now, but I didn't know it then, havin' never been outside my own backyard before.)

So we crossed this Street place, the Old Fella and I. Then we were in another yard with trees and stuff. It was real nice, sorta like our own place. So I stopped to check out the bushes and the grass and the moths and the bugs, and all that good stuff. (Besides, once I saw what the Old Canine was up to, I thought I'd better give him some privacy.) I got to chasin' a big yellow and black flutterby, ya know — runnin' here and there — and then I looked around and, all of a sudden, I was in a strange place all by myself. The Old Fella had gone on home without me.

Well, I'm a big boy now, I thought to myself. I can handle this. But, ya know, suddenly I felt a little bit cold all over, and it wasn't as much fun anymore. But, just to keep things goin' for a bit, I pounced on a few more bugs and chased a shiny blue draggin' fly. Then, I figured I'd better head for home by myself. (Besides, I was gettin' kinda hungry, ya know!)

I started out in what I thought was the right direction, but I couldn't get any place. No matter which way I turned, I was stuck behind this big wire fence. I don't know how I got in there, but I know I just couldn't get myself out. I tried and tried, but I couldn't get around

it. The bottom was sorta buried in the ground, so I couldn't squeeze underneath. The holes between the wires were too small to fit through. And it surely was too big to climb over. Way too big. I was trapped!

I'm kinda ashamed to admit it now, but after tryin' everything I knew, I just sat down and cried. And meowed. And finally, I howled. Oh boy, how I howled! Once I started, I just couldn't stop. All I could think about was gettin' home to my own house. And eatin' outta my own little white bowl. And havin' a cold drink of water. And being with my own family. I was so lonesome and so scared, I howled some more. And then some more. I howled 'til my throat hurt and real tears were runnin' down my face. (And I even had the nose drip, but I honestly wouldn't want anyone to know that!)

Then, in between the howlin' and the meowin' — I heard it. From far away I heard my Mother Person's voice.

"Benjy, Benjy" she was calling. "Where are you?"

That was just the bestest sound in the world. I howled louder and louder hopin' she would hear me. (Truthfully, I was just too scared to stop!)

"Benjy" I heard — and then — "Well I give

up. I just can't find him any where. I'm going indoors."

My heart just thumped and thumped. Would I be stuck here forever?

Then I heard another voice speaking. It was lady who lives in the house next to us. (She shares her life with three Big Tom Cats. I think she must be a very nice person!)

"I think your new kitten is stuck somewhere," she said. "I can hear the little guy just crying his heart out."

"I know," said my Mother Person. "I can hear him too, but I just can't figure out where he is."

Suddenly I found a place between the bushes where I could see through the fence and almost right in front of my eyes, I saw my wonderful Father Person ridin' up and down the street on his bicycle, lookin' all around and callin' me over and over again.

"Benjy, Benjy! Come on out little boy, wherever you are!"

I howled the loudest any little kitten
could ever howl. I howled so loud I made

myself choke. And choke. And, right then, there was Father Person and The Man From Next Door.

"There he is — I see him in behind that old rotten fence across the street."

"Wow! How the heck did he get over there? He could have been killed in all that traffic."

"It looks like he's really stuck!"

(Well, I could have told them that!)

Then the two of them came across the street and pulled and pulled at the bottom of the old fence — and dug with their hands and even with sticks. Finally, just like a miracle, a little space popped open. I squeezed through as fast as I could right up into Father Person's arms and put my claws into his shirt (and into his skin, too, I'm afraid!) and held on for dear life.

"Easy does it , Benjy" he said. "This is a fine kettle of fish!"

"I'll take your bike," said the other Man Person. "You look like you've got your hands full."

I was shakin' and coughin' and chokin' —
and everything. Father Person held me very
tight 'til we got home.

"You'd better take this little guy inside,"
he said to Mother Person. "He looks all
tuckered out."

She took me into the house where it was
cool and quiet. And, to tell the truth, she just
cuddled me and petted me for a long long
time. My throat hurt so bad, I couldn't even
purr. Then she gave me cool water, and
special Tuna Treat cat food (That's my
favorite kind!) and then just a little bit of warm
milk in a saucer.

"That should cure what ails you, little
Benjamin," she said.

Well, that was one time I sure didn't mind
bein' treated like a baby. (Besides, nobody
saw us 'cept for the Old Feline. And she
wouldn't say anythin' anyway!)

But the whole thing sure gave me a lot to
think about. How did somethin' that started
out so good turn into somethin' so bad? But

who knows — maybe there's no answer to a question like that. I think I'll just clean my paws one more time and sleep under here all night, Tomorrow is another day. And I'm not going one step off the back porch, no matter what!

I'm A Big Boy Now -

My Mother Person has this thing she keeps in the kitchen sink. It's round and green and made of plastic, with a zillion little holes in the bottom. When you pour something into it, the solid stuff stays inside the plastic and the juicy stuff goes out through the holes. Father Person usually calls it "that damned drain thing." She says, "it's called a colander, dear." Anyway, I used to be able to sleep in it when I was a kitten and often did, especially when it was nice and warm from the dishwater.

Well, tonight it caught my eye and I tried to climb into it the way I used to. And I just couldn't fit. When I got my head in, my rear end and my tail were hanging out. I didn't think that was so dignified, so I tried again. But when I got all curled up with my tail nicely tucked in, my head was hanging so far over the edge that I had to rest it on a cantaloupe. (Eventually, me and the colander and the cantaloupe all crashed down to the kitchen floor, but that's another story!)

For a while I couldn't figure it out. But then I did. I've grown. I'm big now. I'm just too big to fit into the colander the way I used

to, like I'm too big to fit under the old green chair. (I got stuck in there the other day. It was a very embarrassing experience!) And, ya know, I think I'm almost as big as Gray and Ralphie and Woｒｉｅ, the three huge Tom Cats who live next door. (Truthfully, when I first saw them months and months ago, I was kinda scared. But I'm not scared of them any more. When all is said and done, we've become pretty good friends.)

From what I hear, I'm going to be one year old soon, so I guess I'm not a kitten any more. I guess I'm a Cat. A full grown Cat. Wow! What a mind-boggling thought!

I never really believed the day would come when I would be all grown up, but I guess it finally has. I should have realized it before the business with the colander, but it just sort of slipped up on me. But, all things considered, I've learned so many different things that it doesn't really surprise me too much.

First of all, I know my name, Benjamin, and all my nicknames. Like Ben and Benjy. I know I'm supposed to come right away when my People call me any of those names, and most of the time I do. I know I'm not supposed to go near the road, and most of the time I don't. I know I'm not supposed to go through the hole in the fence, but when Wolfie is outside in his yard, I just can't resist. (Ya know, sometimes Felines just have to communicate with each other in their own private way. It's part of our nature!) But I think my People understand. After I'm out there for a while, one of them usually comes over and scoops me up saying "that's enough visiting for today, kiddo" and carries me home on their shoulders, way up in the air where I can see everything that's going on. I love that.

I know a lot about butterflies and birds and squirrels and mice. I keep trying to catch them. Any one of them. (I haven't succeeded yet, but some day I will. I don't really understand why, but I'm truly determined to do this!) I climb up trees and climb down again without getting stuck. I chase after my ball and retrieve it, which startles everyone. To hear them talk, you'd think I'm the only Feline in the world that does that particular thing. Well, be that as it may, it sure is fun. Father Person throws the ball real hard and makes it bounce off the walls — and I chase it and get it and bring it back to him. Then he pets me and says "good boy, Ben." And that always

makes me feel so fine.

I admit I still have a little trouble with beams of sunlight and black shadows. I keep trying to catch them — and all I come up with is empty air and a bumped nose. And my People laughing at me. But I'll get the hang of it one day. I'm sure I will.

I'm sorry to say, I know all about THE VET. He's the big guy with rubber hands and the white coat who holds me tight and sticks needles into my body. (I just hate him. He scares me to death!) When I see Mother Person getting out the carrying box and I think we might be going to THE VET, I get all shaky and nervous. Do you know what happened one time when she took me to THE VET? He stuck a needle in me and made me sleep for a long, long time. When I woke up I felt kinda strange and dopey. I decided to have a bath and calm myself down. While I was cleaning underneath my tail I found that part of my body was missing. The two little soft/hard bumpy things that had just started to grow back there were absolutely gone. He must have taken them away! Even though my People cuddled me and were very comforting and I heard them say "neutering is for your own good," I will surely hate THE VET 'til the day I die.

Aside from that one monstrous experience, I really have had a very good life up to now. I'm the center of attention in our household most of the time. I've got all I want to eat and drink. I've got my own private Sanitary Arrangement, and it's usually fresh and clean. I've learned to recognize the sounds that mean Mother Person is getting my food bowl out of the closet and getting ready to feed me, so I'm always ready and waiting for her. (She seems to like that.) I know by the squeak when the back door is opening and I might get to go outside and follow Father Person around in the backyard. I've got my choice of nice warm spots to sleep in, toys to play with and loving people to cuddle me.

Ya know, one time Wolfie told me there are Cats who live their entire lives outside in the cold with nobody to feed them and no place to keep warm. They have to steal whatever food they need to eat. And when they're not lucky with the stealing, they sometimes are so hungry their tummies ache and then they get all skinny and starve to death. He said sometimes People throw shoes and sticks and rocks at Cats and try to hurt them, and that Bad Boys tie scarey tin cans to their tails. In fact, Very Bad People have been known to dump Felines out of cars right onto the hard street, leaving them there to get runned over by cars and trucks and be killed. And, worst of all, some Cats never ever have their own People to hold them and cuddle them and play with them. I was so horrified when I heard all this that I didn't dare to go outside my house for days.

Well, now that I'm big and all grown up, I've been seriously thinking over all of this kinda heavy stuff. A mature Fur Person just has to, ya know. And I've come to believe that, when all is said and done, I'm just one lucky guy. I think I better take my responsibilities and my obligations very seriously from now on. Because I want to stay right here in this wonderful world of mine for ever and ever.

Loneliness

Oh, I'm so lonely! I'm as lonely as any kitten could ever be. And I have a big lump inside of me that feels like I swallowed a whole mouse and it got stuck in my throat. But it's not a mouse. It's just some kinda lump of sadness that won't go 'way. I think I might have a broken heart.

See, when I was a very little kitten — only a few weeks old and weighing not much more than two pounds — I came to live in this house. My house. But I wasn't the only Animal here, then. There was an Old Canine and Old Feline. And they were swell. Each of them helped me a lot and taught me important stuff I really needed to know in order to survive.

The Old Canine — his name was Smoke —
was the best. He was black and furry and
very, very big. In the beginning he was
skatey-eighty times bigger than I was.
Honestly, back then my whole self wasn't
even as big as his head — and that included
my tail. And when I was cold or scared or
confused, he used to let me curl up right next
to him and lean against his soft warm fur. I
used to sleep that way almost every single
night. (Deep inside, it felt something like the
days when I used to lie all in a heap with my

litter brothers and sisters, snuggled up with my real birth mother.) I felt so safe and warm, as if nothing bad could ever happen to me if big Smoke was there.

Then, as time went by, the Old Fella got sicker and sicker, and weaker and weaker. He didn't hang out in the back yard with me any more the way he used to. He just went to one certain place and laid there, rain or shine, while I did my own thing. Once in a while he would stand up and bark me if I strayed too far from home. Or maybe he would come over and simply touch me with his nose. But I could see that it took a lot out of him just to do that.

I didn't know exactly what was going on but I could tell that my Mother Person and my Father Person were really upset. They were very quiet and talked very softly to Smoke, and to each other, a lot of the time. Finally one day I heard her say "It's time, dear."

"Maybe next week," he answered. And "thank God we have Benjy to cheer us up."

(Well, even if I didn't understand all of what was going on, that part sounded OK to me.)

Then there came a day when Mother Person went away, and Father Person and another guy got together and tried to put Smoke in the car. Being he was so big and all, they had a hard time of it. I could hear the Old Fella whimpering and crying all the while. (That part was awful!) They were gone for about an hour. When they came back they wouldn't let me go outside with them, so I watched what was happening through the dining room window.

I could see that my old friend was very, very still. He didn't move at all. Not even the littlest bit. They laid him down on the grass way in the back of the backyard and preceded to dig a big hole right next to him. Then they put him into it, wrapped in his favorite hairy blanket, and covered him up with dirt. And they put rocks around on top of the dirt so he could never get out. (I thought that was a terrible thing to do!) And, ya know, I never saw the old guy again after that.

I was considerably upset. And I got really nervous, thinking that if I ever did something wrong — even by mistake — they would put me in the dirt, too. But that didn't happen. Both Mother Person and Father Person hugged me a lot. Sometimes they hugged me so tight

I got the breath squeezed right out of me. But I could tell they were kinda sad, so I didn't even squirm. I just hung out with them and purred as loud as I could 'cause it seemed to please them.

Then, because I was so lonesome for someone to sleep with in the dark night, I tried snuggling up with the Old Feline. Her name was Magnolia and she was one feisty old lady. At first she didn't want me near her, but after a while, especially if the Humans weren't there to see, she would let me cuddle up next to her in the living room chair. She wasn't as soft and warm as Smoke — in fact she was kinda bony — and I had to lie real still cause it hurt her if I moved too fast and bumped into her. But I tried. This went on for awhile, but I knew in my inside heart that something was very wrong. As time went by she just got skinnier and skinner and bonier and bonier. Finally, one day she just stopped eating her food, and stopped using her Sanitary Box, and started to shake and drool and stuff like that. Mother Person held her in her lap all one day and cried and cried. I heard her saying, real softly, "Eighteen years. We had eighteen good years together." And I just stayed under the couch, cause I didn't know what else to do.

Then Father Person took old Maggie out to the car in the special box that we travel in — the one that has a bunch of air holes in it. When they came back, a little while later, I could see that she was very still, too — not moving at all. He dug a little hole in the ground right next to where Smoke's hole is, wrapped her in her old blanket that looks like leopard skin and put her in it. He covered her up with dirt. He did it very gently. And then he put some rocks on the top, just like the other time. And I never saw the old lady again after that minute.

So now I'm the only Animal in this house. I get the very best food in my own dish and clean, cold water two times every day. I play with my ball and my catnip mouse, and I sit in the sun in the kitchen window every morning and watch the squirrels and the birds. And my People play with me and cuddle me and — I think — do the best they can to make me happy. But it's not the same. I sleep by myself, now. And I'm all alone, with none of my own kind. I feel so empty. And so lonely. Am I gonna be sad like this forever? Will the lump inside me ever go away? Some day, will my broken heart get better? I surely do hope so.

A Winter Day

Oh! I'm awake. It's almost daylight and it's a whole new day. I'd better hurry. I've got a million things to do.

First, I've got to stretch, Wow! That makes my fur stand up and my entire body feel good. Now I've got to visit my Sanitary Arrangement. There — that feels good, too. But it looks like I've got some work to do in here, getting things set up just right. I wouldn't want any of my filth to show. Well bred Felines just don't do that.

Okay! That's done. Now I better check around the house and see what's going on. Well, there's not much happening outside the kitchen window. Those lazy birds and squirrels aren't even up yet. Boring creatures! But, look at this. Mother Person's fallen asleep in the big chair with the TV set on. I'd like to wake her up so she can get me my breakfast. But I don't want to get into trouble, so I'll be real gentle. I think I'll just walk up her leg and get into her lap and see what happens.

Hmmm! Not much. Let me try climbing up on her new chair and exercising my nails a bit. Uh oh! I got a swat for that but she still isn't really awake yet. I better try something else. I know. I'll get up here on the top of the chair and knead my paws in her hair. That'll get her up for sure.

"Dammit, Benjamin. Stop it. It's only 5:30 in the morning. Give me a break. It's way too early for breakfast."

Yeah, well, that's what she thinks! But just a minute. Now she's gone into the bedroom and shut the door. Oh rats! There's nothing I can do but wait. Maybe I should check out the kitchen again, in the meantime.

Look at this. Father Person left a big hunk of yummy cake out on the counter. It's the kind with creamy icing on top. I'll just sample it while nobody's around. Now, that's really good. I'll have just another little taste.

And maybe another.

Uh oh! I'd better get outta here. There's feline tongue marks all over the side of the cake. I'm gonna get in trouble for sure. Maybe if I push it to the edge of the counter, and it falls over, it'll smash up real good and they'll never know I've been licking the icing.

What a crash! That'll get her up for sure. Yup. I can hear her stirring around. I'll just wait right here by the bedroom door like I've been here for ages. I'm gonna put on my most patient and devoted look, ya know.

"What was that big crash? Was that you, Benjy? Are you okay?"

She follows me while I hold my tail up in it's highest and proudest position and walk very, very slowly down the hall to the kitchen. My most dignified power walk. I practice it every day.

"Dammit Ben. Can't you please go a little faster? You do this silly business every morning. You're going to make me step on you if you keep it up."

Uh oh! Now Mother Person's going to

see the smashed plate and the mushed up cake.

"What a mess. Helluva way to start the day."

Then she mutters some other things to herself. It begins to look as if she's more angry at Father Person for leaving the cake out on the counter than at me for knocking it down. That's cool! In the meantime, she reaches into the pantry and gets out a can of my favorite cat food and my very own brown dish.

"Catfish flavor this morning, Ben. Okay?"

While she dishes it out I purr a whole lot and I rub the side of my jaw on the can, on the dish and on her hand. That's because they're all mine. Mine! Mine! Mine! And then she pets me all over, scratches my head and puts the dish full of delicious smelly catfish in my own special eating corner. Yum yum! I eat every bit, right down to the bottom.

I'm so busy eating that I don't pay attention to anything else. I know Mother Person fills my white dish with clean, cold water — because she always does — and my red dish with enough dry, crunchy food to last the rest of the day. Boy, I'm one lucky guy! I guess she also cleans up the broken dish and the smashed cake, 'cause when I look again that mess is all gone.

Well, I believe in doing things in proper order. There's a time and a place for everything. All felines know that. And now it's the exact time for a big all-over bath. I think I'll do it in the parlor by the wood stove. Father Person's got a big blaze going and it's nice and warm there. In fact, it's so warm that I think, when I'm all clean, I'll just stay right there for my morning nap.

"My goodness, that kitten sure can sleep. It's mid-afternoon and he's been snoozing by the fire since breakfast. He's really got the life!"

Afternoon? I can't believe I've slept that long. I'd better get up and doing. I'll just wash my face real quick and get myself together. Now, on to the kitchen table. I know I shouldn't be up here but it's the best place for looking out into the yard. Goodness! Look at those squirrels. It makes my teeth chatter when I see them scooting up and down my trees, in my yard. Maybe I better go out and chase a few, just to let them know I'm really the Cat In Charge, here.

"What's up, Ben? Why are you jumping around like that? Do you want to go out? Is that it? OK — but it's really cold out there. Watch that you don't freeze your feet."

The cold bricks sting my footpads but I run over them as fast as I can and sit on the big rock. It's usually nice and warm from the sunshine. But would you just look at this. Now that I've finally got myself situated, the blasted squirrels have taken off. Well, I see a gang of birds around the birdfeeder that I could chase, but — to tell you the truth — I'm giving up on them. Every time I get myself all hunkered down and ready to spring, they fly away and I'm out there looking like a jerk. I strut around and make believe I wasn't really trying to get one, but I think my People can tell. Sometimes they laugh at me. I'll just have to do some more of my power walk and show everybody I'm the genuine and only Cat of the House.

I guess I should check out the mouse holes back by the compost heap, but that's so far and the grass is all icy. Maybe I just better go back inside. It's almost time for Mother Person to start cooking dinner. She might even be doing something to a chicken. If I'm lucky, I might even get the liver. I'd better get in there and check it out.

Wow! I'm tired. I supervised the whole dinner. Mother Person let me have the chicken liver, all nice and warm from the oven. Then I got my ball and brought it to Father Person. He throws it and I fetch it, over and over and over again until I'm all tired out. Finally I put it down where he can't get it without getting up from his chair. He really understands what that means.

"Had enough, Ben? Want to quit?"

I go over by his feet and hang around. I put the ball into his slipper. I get closer and closer. In a little while, I climb into his lap. He dozes off and let's me stay there. I purr and purr. I'm warm and happy right down to the place where my heart beats.

"Damned cat sounds like a motor boat!"

"Well, Pop — it isn't any louder than your snoring."

It's all dark outside now. The day is almost over. When they go into the study to watch the TV, I climb into Mother Person's lap. I fall asleep again. In a little while she moves me onto the couch. She's very gentle. I hardly even wake up. In fact, I don't really get up until the new day comes.

When Lili Came

We were in our country house when Lili came. It wasn't a total surprise to me. I had heard Mother Person talking on the phone to almost everyone.

"And he said he'd never have a second cat," she told one of her friends "because of his allergies. Said if I loved him, I'd never want another. Said if I ever got another cat, he'd be gone. What a hoot!"

I knew she was talking about Father Person, but so what. She had said those interesting words: "another cat." Was Father Person bringing another Feline into our family? Was I going to have a friend? Would it be someone I'd be able to love? Would it be a real pal like Wolfie or Gray? Or just some low class stray off the streets? Well, time will tell.

Finally, Father Person showed up one
evening with this little waifling on his
shoulder. A mostly-white Calico female, tiny

and delicate. Little feet. Slanty yellow eyes. Fluffy. And feisty. Right off the bat, she didn't take any guff from me, and I was more than twice her size. When I first saw her across the room I sounded my loudest feline war cry — and she sounded back, almost as loud. Even tho' she was very skinny and looked half-starved, she wasn't afraid. She laid her ears back and slunk down to the floor in the attack position, the way we do. "Well, at least she's no scaredy-cat" I thought to myself.

We both hissed and spit and growled and whacked front paws and everything, putting on a fierce show for our People. To tell the truth, I think they only laughed at us, but we did our best for about two days. (Honestly, I found it all rather tiring!) Mother Person fed us in separate places and was careful to pet us equally. But she always gave me my food before Lili got hers. That's only proper, given my position as First Cat of the House.

I kept watching this feline interloper. Her presence was making me very nervous. I spent a lot of time in the closet, peeking out, trying to see what she was doing. And, ya know, she simply went about her business, checking everything out and stuff like that.

(Sometimes I thought she was peeking me too, but I wasn't sure.)

But, while I was watching, I kept seeing how pretty she was. And how graceful. And, ya know, sometimes I thought she seemed awfully puzzled, like she didn't really know what was going on. First of all, I could see she didn't understand that, in this household, we always eat two times a day, no matter what. She gulped down her breakfast so fast she almost got sick. And then just looked and looked when we got our night food, but didn't touch it 'til after everyone went to sleep. Ya know, maybe she didn't have it so good in the-wherever-she-was before she came here.

Well, after the second day, when she hissed me for getting into her personal space — I did the polite thing and walked away backwards. I did that twice. Now, if she knows anything at all, she'll know I mean her no harm!

On the third day, I was so moved by her kittenish ways that I leaned over and kissed her on that cute brown spot on the bridge of her nose. I guess she didn't understand that I wanted to be friends. Actually, she almost jumped out of her skin. She looked so scared.

After a few seconds she remembered to hiss-and-spit me right in my face, but I could see she wasn't really angry. I think it's more a case of not knowing the correct thing to do. (Ya know — she hasn't had a lot of training. Sometimes I think she doesn't even know her

own name. Isn't that embarrassing?) I'll just have to be patient and try to teach her by example. I won't try to kiss her any more. I'll continue to be The Perfect Gentleman Cat — not showing off, or anything — just letting her know that, around here, things are to be correctly done.

On the fourth morning she woke me up, and when I was still a little dopey and dreamy, she chased me up and down the stairs. Well, when I got myself together I chased her right back. Up and down. And behind the cushions on the couch. And under the dining room table.

"Wow!" yelled Father Person, just coming out of the shower. "It's a zoo around here!"

Just to show him what's what and who's in charge, I jumped six feet into the air and right over the wooden cat statue that I hate. Pow! I haven't had that much fun in ages!

Day and days have passed. Father Person has gone back to the city. Lili has gained a lot of weight — four whole pounds. She still is tiny and delicate, but getting stronger every day. She can tight-rope-walk on the very edge of the balcony because her feet are so little. (I can't do that.) She can sit her entire body on the narrow window sill. (I can't do that. I'm too big. I fall off.) She can climb right straight up the window screen when she's on the porch chasing bugs. (I can't do that, either.) She's really something else! And, ya know, I think she's beginning to feel at home.

Sometimes I think it might be better to be an Only Cat. So far, this no-account little piece of stray cat fluff has taken over my favorite window sill. And my second favorite window sill. She's taken to sleeping in the box of computer paper on the shelf by Mother Person's desk. (And that used to be mine exclusively!) Then, in the middle of the night, when Mother Person fell fast asleep in the big chair by the TV set, she even tried to take over her lap. Mother Person woke up when I shrieked.

"Heavens, Ben!" she said. Then — "Alright. You look absolutely mournful." And she put the little brat right down on the floor. Very firmly. (Let me tell you, she hasn't tried that trick again!)

But just this morning, when I was cuddled up in bed with Mother Person, I rolled over and felt this other furry body. There she was again in one of my special, private places. I woke right up. So did Lili. Finding ourselves practically face-to-face like that, neither of us knew quite what to do — so we chased up and down the stairs for awhile and made an enormous rumpus. Mother Person woke up and fed us, even tho' it wasn't even six o'clock in the morning.

Now, I'm dozing and thinking in the biggest chair. (She's in the computer paper box, but I can live with it!) I wonder — why do I keep watching her all the time? I can't keep my eyes off her. And when my People took her to The Vet, why was I so worried? I almost died of anxiety. I knew he would stick needles into her body and squeeze her tummy and put sticky drops up her nose — and he did. When she came home she was confused and scared and tired. I felt so sorry for her that I kissed her on the nose again. (Oh, I know I wasn't going to, but I just couldn't help it!) Anyway, this time she let me. And she even kissed me back. Just one little lick. Of course, I stayed near her when she was trying to sleep off the entire horrible experience. And she let me. And then, after she got up, I let her eat right out of my dish for the first time. (Yes, that's right. My very own dish with my own entire name on it.)

Ya know — I kinda liked feeling Lili's furry little body next to mine in the bed. It made me feel not so lonesome any more. I don't have that dead-mouse-stuck-in-my-throat feeling that I used to have. I groom my fur a lot so I look my best at all times. And I sit up as tall as I can, right in that bar of sunlight that makes my whiskers shine. And, last night when we had visitors, Lili and I played the greatest cat games — over the table and the kitchen counter and around everybody's feet — 'til someone said "Aren't they just beautiful together!"

Well, maybe she really doesn't even know her name yet, and maybe she does scratch the easy chair sometimes and drink out of the toilet, but nobody's perfect.

To tell the truth, I think I'm in love. I really do.

Lili's Story

Huh! He thinks he's so great, that Benjamin. He think he rules this house and can do everything just the way he wants it. Whenever he wants it. Well, maybe being First Cat and all, he's entitled to some special privileges — but not everything.

I know he thinks I'm just a stray — a nobody from nowhere. But that's not so. I am somebody. And I did once have people and places of my own. (It's just that, now that things are getting so wonderful, I'm beginning to dis-remember them a little.) Besides, some parts of my life are so yucky-awful I don't ever want to tell that high-and-mighty Benjy about them. And sometimes, just thinking about things that happened to me in the past makes my brain hurt.

See — I'm just like every other cat. Once

I had a Real Feline Mother and a bunch of litter brothers and sisters. I think I was the smallest one. One of the Children of that House named me "Runty." I didn't like that so much but at least I did have a name like a respectable house cat. Then, one day, they just passed me on to another family. Just like that. These new People lived in a place called The Bron-ix in New York City. It was a poor kind of place. Not even a house with a yard — just a 'partment. Actually, it was dirty and there were lots of fleas and roach bugs in it. (I know that's pretty yucky but, in a way, it was fun. Chasing them roaches and getting them and crunching them in the middle of the night! Wow!)

There was a Father Person and a Boy Person who were really nice. They cuddled me whenever they could, called me by my name and gave me little treats. But the Mother Person was mean. She never petted me and always yelled and talked about money. She kept saying they didn't have enough money to buy proper cat food, so she fed me scraps. Sometimes it was rotten and smelled and tasted just awful! I couldn't really eat it so I was almost always hungry. Maybe that's why I never really grew up and am still so little. She never gave me any milk or water so I had to drink out of the toilet. (That's an old Feline survival trick!) And, this is so embarrassing! — I didn't even have my own Sanitary Arrangement. I had to go outside the 'partment and find a spot in the smelly old hallway. Gross!

Anyway, one day the Boy noticed how the fleas made me itch and scratch, so he spent all the money he had for a flea collar. He put it around my neck. I was so proud. Until the Mother saw it. She got really angry and started screaming at the Boy and even at the Father. The Father was sitting at the kitchen table. He put his head down and said "Okay. Okay. I'll get rid of her."

The Boy just cried and cried and held me very tight. I really didn't understand all that was happening, but I knew, in my heart of hearts, that it wasn't any good.

A few days later, the Father took me out of the 'partment in a cardboard box. We went in a car to a far, far place where there was grass and trees. Then he kissed me and hugged me and put me down on the grass and said "Life is tough. Good Luck, little kitty."

Then he got into the car and slammed the door and went away and LEFT ME FLAT. I didn't know where I was and I didn't have any food or water or anybody or anything.

That's about the worst thing that can happen to a cat! In just one instant I went from a respectable house cat to a no-account alley cat. A homeless stray. Now, you tell me — what does that uppity Benjamin know about the real world? He's been with this same wonderful family all his life and has had simply everything he could ever want since he was a tiny kitten. You'd think he could have a little sympathy and understanding for those who aren't so lucky?

Well, anyway, I walked around and around this big grassy field. I was so hungry I thought my insides would stick together. I tried to catch birds and mice to eat but, being a city cat and having never ever done that before in my life, I didn't have any luck. I drank some rainwater out of a puddle after a big storm. (I hid under the bushes but I got soaked anyway!) After my flea collar got wet it seemed to get smaller and smaller. It was so tight I was choking. Boy oh boy — was I scared! I didn't know whether I would starve to death or choke to death. I stayed under a bush all through one dark night and cried and howled as loud as I could, but nobody came to help me. (To tell you the truth, I think that was when I lost the first of my nine lives!)

When the daytime came, I went out into the sunlight to get warm. I was shivering from the cold and was almost too weak to walk. Then — far away — I saw a Boy coming towards me. He was riding a bike. And right behind him was a tall, skinny old man with a white beard, carrying something made out of paper and string. I heard him say, "Get off that bike, kiddo, and let's fly this kite."

I kept my eyes on the little boy and went towards him as fast as I could. I was staggering with weakness and kept falling down — but I just kept on trying. The boy got off his bike and ran towards me.

"Grandpa," he was shouting. "Look. A kitty! A little lost kitty." He knelt down and held me close. "Grandpa, she likes me," he said. "Listen how loud she's purring." And then, without even asking the old man, he opened this funny looking bottle and poured something into the cup that was also the cover. Milk. Delicious milk made extra sweet with brown stuff. He let me drink the whole cupful and then gave me another. I was delirious with pleasure.

"Grandpa," said the boy, "she drank it all up. But I think she's still hungry. Look how she's winding herself around my feet. And hear how she's crying. She's so skinny. I think she's almost starving to death."

Well, as it happened, that was to be the

First Day of the Rest of My Lives! The old man, who is now my Father Person, took me to a nice warm house that smelled of Cat. First he cut off my flea collar so I could breathe and swallow correctly. Then he opened can after can of food and let me eat until I was full. (I think I ate three whole cans. One of them was real tuna.) Then he showed me an excellent Sanitary Arrangement and let me go to sleep on a little green rug by the kitchen sink.

(Actually, I didn't ever want to leave this kitchen if I could help it. That was where all the cat food cans were stacked up. I never saw so many in my whole life and I wasn't ready to let them out of my sight.)

I was sorry to see the little boy leave, but he had to go back to his own house. Anyway it was nice and peaceful — just me and Father Person. He fed me and gave me milk and always kept a dish full of clean, cool water on the kitchen floor. He let me sleep in his lap and he talked to me from time to time. When he went away, I roamed all over this big, comfortable house — checked out all the rooms and beds and cubbies. It was simply beautiful. And I could tell another Feline lived there.

Then, one day, Father Person scooped me up and took me with him in a car. Boy — was I scared! I thought: "maybe he's going to drop me in another strange place and leave me to starve." I admit it — I cried a little. And when I did, he picked me up and let me ride in his lap, looking out the window, for the rest of the trip. That was nifty — just watching the world go by. Then we got to where we are now. A little cottage on a big hill. With all the food and water and milk and treats that any cat could ever want. And a big screened in porch where I can watch birds and stuff. (Actually, I've been catching some real fast Daddy-Long-Legs. They really give you a good chase! It's fun!)

The best — and worst — part of it all is that big, handsome Benjamin. He's absolutely the most beautiful Feline I've ever seen. But he's bossy and snotty and thinks he knows just everything. (To tell you the truth, I don't think he's ever seen a roach! Or ever been hungry! Well, I shouldn't hate him for that.)

When I first got here, he made Feline War cries at me. Well, I wasn't a New York City street kitty for nothing. I made my own War Cry, just as loud as I could. (Frankly, I think he seemed impressed.) Then he spent two or three days pouting and sulking, hiding inside this big closet and peeking me. Well, I admit it. I was peeking him too, but I tried not to let him catch me at it.

Now things have settled down. This Mother Person is really nice, but I'm afraid to love her just yet. I have to watch and see, in case she turns out to be mean like the last one. She calls me Lili. It's not my real name so I don't answer — but maybe one day soon I will. Sometimes the Boy comes to see me. We play paper-and-string and I follow him everywhere. When he sleeps over, I cuddle in his bed.

And that Benjy. He thinks he's fooling me, acting tough, but I can tell he's beginning to love me. A lot. Every once in a while he gets wild and fresh with me — jumps on me and bites my neck. But, I'm faster than he is, and when I hiss-and-spit right in his face and lay my ears back and show my fang teeth, he backs away and leaves me alone. (Maybe he's not as brave as he looks!) Then, he tries to sneak close to me when I'm sleeping, but I'm not letting him get away with that yet. I keep sleeping in his precious old computer paper box just to get his goat. Tough on him.

Maybe when he learns to treat me with respect, and stops telling me how to behave correctly and it's not nice to drink out of the toilet, I might let him love me some more. I might even love him back a little bit, myself.

After all, he is very big. And very handsome.

Afterword

I am writing this on Benjamin's eighth birthday.

He's no longer a kitten — but probably the largest, most stately cat you have ever seen.

He's an ounce or two short of 30 pounds and reminds me of the largest, best looking kid on the high school football team. Huge. Awesome. Intimidating. Not fat. Just big. Because of a medical anomaly one of his ears is now chronically bent, giving him a "tough guy" appearance. And he can be as tough as he looks.

Lili, on the other hand, remains minute. Though now filled out to a comfortable roundness, she is but a fraction of his size but nonetheless rules his life. She tantalizes him, turning over on her back and reaching for him with her dainty paws until he attempts to respond. As soon as he reaches out to touch her, she hisses and spits in his face and runs into a cubby or a corner where he cannot follow because he's simply too big. This game is played out several times daily. Sometimes they go to war over a patch of sun on the dining room floor or a breezy window sill. To the uninitiated, the noise they make is frightening and their actions may appear hostile and frenzied. But the rules of engagement are ritualistic and unvarying. Lili always wins. It's big Benjamin who wears the scratches on his nose.

During the past summer we were

vacationing, as usual, in our cottage in Kintnersville, Pennsylvania — the tiniest and most bucolic of towns. I headed home for an overnight visit with Jim, became extremely ill and was hospitalized for many, many months here in New York. The cats were lovingly cared for by our wonderful Bucks County neighbor, Margie Barnett. They met and became friends with her four cats and her old dogs — and spent untold hours on the screened-in sun porch, catching bugs and watching wild critters. (Lili even had a pet hoptoad small enough to fit under the screen door. She never hurt him — only watched his

progress until her eyes crossed.)

As our time apart stretched on, I was beset by the fear that they would forget me. But of course they didn't. Within minutes of their return, our routines resumed as if there had been no interruption. After a standoffish period, lasting perhaps fifteen seconds, Benjy was in my lap, purring his heart out — and Lili was going about her self-appointed catly chores. Devoted "Aunt Margie" and the country life was set aside for the moment as if it had never happened. The entire experience tucked away somewhere in their amazing feline brains, to be taken out and used again at the proper time.

And now?

I am physically much slower and weaker than I was before — and significantly crippled. Without my two furry feline friends, I might have become desolate. But they keep me company, day and night. Their never-ending antics cheer me.

Benjamin has become the most highly evolved animal I have ever known. How he did it is a mystery to me — but his understanding of human vocabulary is extensive. I believe he knows at least 50 spoken words. He is moody and, from time to time, gets depressed. He signifies this by standing with his back to the room and staring at the wall. When he wants peace and quiet, and wishes to be left alone, he covers his closed eyes with his paws. He has been known to watch TV — but only if there are cats in the story.

His internal clock is set for 6:30 AM and 4 PM precisely. At 6:30 he wakes me up, "power walks" me down the hall to the kitchen and demands that I prepare his breakfast. At 4 PM his tummy tells him it is time for me to set out his evening meal. (He doesn't always eat the food — just has a driving need to see me make it ready for him according to his rigid personal schedule.) At all other times, he is wherever I am. (As I write this, he is dozing in one of the file drawers in my desk. There is no way he could get any closer.) A friend of mine has described our relationship as a "classic case of over-bonding." That could very well be.

Lili, on the other hand, spends her day as close to Jim as he will allow her to be. We both believe that — since he saved her life — she thinks she owes him her soul. To see her sitting on a whirling lathe or drill press when he is involved in his woodshop is, to most people, a frightening sight. But Lili is not frightened at all. If you get close enough, you'll find she's purring like a motor boat — her slanted yellow-green eyes half closed in contentment.

Because of increasing vehicular traffic here on Long Island and the danger it presented, they both have had to become house cats. But it is a big house and their play space is considerable. They do not appear at all unhappy in their world.

The first chapbook "Benjamin's World" was printed in 1991 and re-printed again in the same year by Anderie Poetry Press in Easton, Pennsylvania. Changes in technology made the original type obsolete so there could be no third version. And there were more stories to tell about these remarkable felines and our life together — hence this new enhanced edition.

So here we are. It's 1998 and the cast of characters remains essentially the same. I tell our story with love. And dedicate it with heartfelt gratitude to our Bucks County family: "Aunt Margie," the rest of the neighborhood gang and all the Kintnersville Critters.

(Skeeter, Jesse, and Barnaby — the felines.
Pasha, Obie, and Mica — the equines. Rebel —
the new canine. Junior the rooster. The ten
Polish hens. And especially, to Tono, Julie,
Matthew and Teal — the loving memories.)

Shari Nocks Gladstone
aka "Mother Person"
Dix Hills, N.Y.
3/29/98

It's also time to say a special thanks to
Ms. Joanne Greig for a lifetime of friendship,
as well as for her total understanding,
expertise and assistance with all the
often-confusing "newfangled" computer
technology.

And to Candace Staulcup, artist. Her
warm and lovely illustrations within these
pages speak for themselves.

Pussy Cat Heaven

...an addendum

This endpaper is especially for those of my friends who have loved a pet and lost it. So sad. It doesn't matter if it was a cat, dog, pony, horse, bird, hamster or fish. It could be any of the little critters we've loved and cared for and who have, unconditionally, loved us back. Given how long most of us have lived we are, perhaps, talking about several or many pets. Yet, each loss is as gut-wrenching as the first.

Listen to me. Rest easy. They are all in heaven. Puppy heaven. Kitty heaven. Whatever. I'll call it Pussy Cat heaven for now, but you know what I mean.

Let me describe it.

It's vast and ever so beautiful. The weather is always just as one would wish. There is grass, trees, clear blue sky and puffy clouds. There are meadows with sun-warmed rocks to lie on and lovely bushes for noonday shelter. Stables where the doors are always open and the hay in the mangers forever fresh and sweet. Big wooden dog houses with fresh straw for bedding and even favorite earthtime blankets and toys. All of the furry pet people who have passed from earth are there and, miraculously, all their aches and pains are gone. They romp as they once did. Their fur shines. Their ears are perky. Their noses are cold and wet. Their eyes are bright. They are eternally in the prime of their lives. There are many species here. They all get along. There are no fights. Old earth pals touch noses in greeting. New friends are everywhere.

Now I must ask you a question. Have you, on occasion, seen something out of the corner of your eye that made you think of your long-gone pussy cat? A shred of movement? A shadow? A sensation? A feeling that the very air around you has moved?

You quickly turn your head, but there's really nothing there. And you say to yourself

— or perhaps only think — oh! just for a
moment I thought I saw my old Magnolia. Or
Julie. Or Smoke.

Well — you surely did!

As we loved our pets so did they love us. Even in heaven, they think about us now and again, and are concerned about our well being. They miss us. Is she taking her walks without me, one might think. Or, who is sleeping in the bed when the nights are cold. Or, who is barking to warn her when the bad people come.

As they think of us so we think of them. To this day, when I open the front door I say (or think) don't let Smoke out. And when it's time to go upstairs for the night, I still look for Magnolia so that we can play our favorite game, first up to bed.

But so magical is pussy cat heaven that, when they want to, they can momentarily pass through the gossamer barriers and look in on us. Just for a second. Just for a heartbeat. To assure themselves that all is well. (We may only be able to do this in our thoughts, but they can really do it. Believe me!)

I think that's what we see when the air moves. I'd like to think that's what we see. It comforts me to think that's what we see.

(This piece was especially written for the North Shore Women's Newspaper, Huntington, Long Island, N.Y. where Ms. Gladstone writes the column, "Never Too Old.")